# SUMMARY OF NEVER BE SICK AGAIN

*Access Supernatural Health Through Jesus" Resurrection Power*

## CHAD GONZALES

Copyright 2024–Harrison House

All rights reserved. This book is protected by the copyright laws of the United States of America. This book may not be copied or reprinted for commercial gain or profit. The use of short quotations or occasional page copying for personal or group study is permitted and encouraged. Permission will be granted upon request. Unless otherwise indicated, all scripture quotations are taken from the *King James Version* of the Bible. Used by permission. All rights reserved.

All emphasis within Scripture quotations is the author's own. Please note that Harrison House's publishing style capitalizes certain pronouns in Scripture that refer to the Father, Son, and Holy Spirit, and may differ from some publishers' styles. Take note that the name satan and related names are not capitalized. We choose not to acknowledge him, even to the point of violating grammatical rules.

Harrison House P.O. Box 310, Shippensburg, PA 17257-0310

This book and all other Harrison House's books are available at Christian bookstores and distributors worldwide.

For Worldwide Distribution.

Reach us on the Internet: www.harrisonhouse.com.

ISBN 13 TP: 978-1-6675-1004-0

ISBN 13 eBook: 978-1-6675-1005-7

# CONTENTS

| | |
|---|---|
| Introduction | v |
| 1. In the Garden | 1 |
| 2. Delivered from Egypt | 5 |
| 3. Healing Under the Old Covenant | 9 |
| 4. A Better Covenant | 13 |
| 5. The Covenant of Grace | 17 |
| 6. The True Gospel of Healing | 21 |
| 7. The Real Meaning of 1 Peter 2:24 | 25 |
| 8. The Day You Became Alive | 29 |
| 9. Made Perfect | 33 |
| 10. Filled with Life | 36 |
| 11. The Flow in You | 39 |
| 12. Who Do You Think You Are? | 43 |
| 13. Receiving Your Healing is for the Sinner | 47 |
| 14. You Are the Body of Christ | 51 |
| 15. Don't Get Cheated | 55 |
| 16. Our Belief in Sickness | 59 |
| 17. A New Kingdom | 63 |
| 18. Substituting Brass for Gold | 66 |
| 19. Generational Curses and Your Bloodline | 70 |
| 20. Satan Isn't Trespassing on Your Body | 73 |
| 21. Whatever Has Your Imagination Has Your Faith | 77 |
| 22. Stay Connected to the Source | 80 |
| 23. When Christians Are Sick | 84 |
| 24. Accidents and Injuries | 87 |
| 25. Food and Drugs | 91 |
| About the Publisher | 95 |

# INTRODUCTION

*Never Be Sick Again* explores a profound yet simple truth: through Christ, believers have been granted the divine promise of health and wholeness. This revolutionary book challenges traditional perspectives on sickness and health, offering biblical insights that empower readers to walk in divine health as a reflection of their covenant with God. It calls Christians to shift their focus from managing illness to living in the fullness of their union with Christ.

In its pages, the author emphasizes that sickness is not merely a natural occurrence but often the result of spiritual, emotional, and physical misalignment. Rooted in scripture and supported by practical examples, the book unpacks essential principles of faith, spiritual authority, and the believer's identity in Christ. It underscores how proper stewardship of the body, disciplined thought life, and abiding in God's presence can lead to a life free from sickness.

## INTRODUCTION

This summary condenses the book's life-changing teachings into actionable insights while preserving its original intent and message. Each chapter builds on the foundational truths of God's provision for health, tackling topics like the power of imagination, the importance of self-control, and practical steps for aligning with God's will for our physical and spiritual well-being.

As you engage with this summary, be prepared to rethink old paradigms, embrace new perspectives on health, and take practical steps toward a life marked by divine health. Let this journey into *Never Be Sick Again* inspire you to fully embrace the abundant life that God has designed for His children.

# CHAPTER 1

# IN THE GARDEN

## Bible Verse

Genesis 1:26-28 NKJV "Then God said, 'Let Us make man in Our image, according to Our likeness; let them have dominion over the fish of the sea, over the birds of the air, and over the cattle, over all the earth and over every creeping thing that creeps on the earth.' So God created man in His own image; in the image of God He created him; male and female He created them. Then God blessed them, and God said to them, 'Be fruitful and multiply; fill the earth and subdue it; have dominion over the fish of the sea, over the birds of the air, and over every living thing that moves on the earth.'"

## Introduction

Chapter 1 of "Never Be Sick Again" delves into the biblical account of creation, emphasizing the special role and divine qualities bestowed upon humanity. It describes how, from the beginning, humans were intended to live in health, mirroring God's image and vitality.

## Word of Wisdom

*"As it is for God in Heaven, it was to be that way for man on the earth."*

## Main Theme

The chapter illustrates God's original plan for mankind to live free of sickness and in dominion over creation, a state altered by Adam's sin which introduced death and decay into the world.

## Key Points

God created all life with the inherent ability to reproduce after its own kind, setting mankind apart by making them in His own image.

Mankind was endowed with God's spiritual substance, meant to shield them from disease and death.

The fall of Adam introduced sin into the world, disrupting the divine flow of life and subjecting humanity to mortality and suffering.

Despite the fall, God's design included a complex immune system as a testament to His mercy, preparing humanity for survival outside Eden.

The immune system, though remarkable, was a contingency plan, highlighting God's foreknowledge and provision.

The ultimate restoration of life and dominion was set in motion through the promise of salvation in Jesus Christ.

## Key Themes

- **Divine Image and Authority:** Humanity was uniquely created in the image of God, endowed with the authority to rule over creation. This divine likeness was intended to manifest as complete health and eternal life, mirroring God's own immortality.
- **Impact of Sin:** The narrative clearly delineates how sin not only affected spiritual communion with God but had tangible effects on human health and the natural world. Death entered, and with it, all forms of disease and decay, showcasing the severe consequences of disobedience.
- **God's Provision through the Immune System:** Even in judgment, God's mercy was evident in the complexity of the human immune system, designed to protect against the diseases that would emerge post-Eden. This system reflects God's intricate design and care for humanity, even in a fallen state.
- **Salvific Promise:** The chapter points to the hope embedded in Genesis 3:15, where the promise of Jesus Christ introduces the potential for restoration to God's original design for health and life, highlighting the messianic prophecy as the pivotal solution to the problem of sin and death.
- **Theological Implications of Humanity's Role:** There is a deep theological exploration of what it means to be made in the image of God and how this status was impacted by the Fall. The

discussion reveals the balance between free will, divine sovereignty, and the ongoing redemptive plan of God.

## Conclusion

"In the Garden" sets a foundational understanding of humanity's intended state versus its fallen condition, emphasizing that through Jesus Christ, there is a promise of return not only to spiritual righteousness but also to the wholeness of life as God originally intended. This chapter reassures us of God's eternal plan for our complete restoration, both spiritually and physically.

## CHAPTER 2

## DELIVERED FROM EGYPT

### Bible Verse

Exodus 12:13 NKJV "Now the blood shall be a sign for you on the houses where you are. And when I see the blood, I will pass over you; and the plague shall not be on you to destroy you when I strike the land of Egypt."

### Introduction

"Delivered from Egypt" recounts the biblical story of the Passover, highlighting God's miraculous intervention in freeing the Israelites from Egyptian bondage. The chapter explores how this event prefigures the ultimate deliverance from sin and disease through Jesus Christ.

### Word of Wisdom

*"Not one single Israelite left Egypt weak or sick, and even the elderly people had their youth renewed!"*

## Main Theme

The chapter focuses on the night of the Passover as a monumental event of mass healing and divine preparation for the Israelites' journey from slavery to the Promised Land, reflecting the comprehensive salvation that comes through faith.

## Key Points

- The Passover represents the most significant mass healing event in biblical history, where every Israelite was healed.
- This event symbolized the future sacrifice of Christ, the Lamb who takes away the sin of the world.
- God's deliverance of the Israelites from Egypt serves as a type and shadow of Christian salvation.
- The miracle of the Passover underscores God's power not only to heal but also to protect and provide.
- The covenant God established with Israel promised health and protection as long as they remained obedient.

## Key Themes

- **Symbolism of the Passover Lamb:** The Passover lamb was a prophetic symbol of Jesus Christ, whose future sacrifice would bring about healing and salvation for mankind. Eating the lamb led to

immediate physical healing for the Israelites, foreshadowing the spiritual and physical healing available through Christ.
- **Comprehensive Divine Intervention:** The chapter elaborates on how God's intervention during the Passover was not limited to spiritual salvation but included physical healing, provision, and protection, showcasing His holistic care for His people.
- **Covenant Relationship and Divine Health:** God's promise to the Israelites included a life free from diseases common in Egypt, contingent upon their obedience. This reflects the broader biblical theme that God desires to be not only the Savior but also the Healer.
- **Significance of Obedience:** The text highlights the conditional aspect of God's promises, where the health and prosperity of the Israelites depended on their adherence to His commands. This theme teaches that spiritual obedience has tangible benefits.
- **Legacy of Faith and Provision:** The narrative connects the physical deliverance from Egypt with the spiritual deliverance provided by Jesus, emphasizing that faith in God carries powerful, real-world implications, including health and protection.

## Conclusion

"Delivered from Egypt" vividly portrays the miraculous night of the Passover as a transformative event for the Israelites, setting the stage for their journey towards a promised relationship with God that ensured their health and prosperity. The chapter reiterates the powerful bond between divine promise and human obedience, which remains a cornerstone of faith and is as relevant today as it was during the Exodus.

## CHAPTER 3

# HEALING UNDER THE OLD COVENANT

**Bible Verse**

Deuteronomy 7:15 NKJV "And the Lord will take away from you all sickness, and will afflict you with none of the terrible diseases of Egypt which you have known, but will lay them on all those who hate you."

**Introduction**

"Healing Under the Old Covenant" delves into the conditional promises of health and prosperity that God made to the Israelites, contingent on their obedience to His commands as outlined in Deuteronomy 7.

**Word of Wisdom**

*"As long as you do not sin, sickness can't touch you." Chad Gonzales*

## Main Theme

This chapter explores the profound connection between obedience to God's laws and the health benefits promised to the Israelites under the Old Covenant, emphasizing the spiritual and physical implications of their obedience.

## Key Points

- God promised removal of sickness and abundant blessings as rewards for obedience.
- The blessings included fertility for families and livestock, and freedom from all sickness.
- The conditions set by God were clear: obey and live in health, or disobey and suffer curses, including disease.
- The Old Covenant served to highlight humanity's need for a Savior and foreshadowed the coming of Jesus Christ.
- Under the Old Covenant, the health of the Israelites was directly linked to their spiritual obedience.

## Key Themes

- **Conditional Health Promises:** The Old Covenant outlined that the health and prosperity of the Israelites were conditional upon their adherence to God's commands. These promises were a continuation of God's original intention for mankind to live without sickness, as stated in Genesis.

- **Spiritual Obedience and Physical Health:** This theme underscores the integral link between spiritual obedience and physical health, suggesting that living according to God's laws naturally leads to a life free from diseases known in Egypt, thereby setting the Israelites apart from other nations.
- **The Role of Sin in Sickness:** The chapter posits that sin is the root cause of sickness; thus, avoiding sin equates to avoiding disease. This premise forms the basis for the health directives given by God to the Israelites.
- **Foreshadowing Christ's Redemption:** The conditions of the Old Covenant highlight humanity's inability to fully comply with God's laws and the consequent need for a perfect Savior. This sets the stage for the New Covenant under Jesus Christ, which offers grace and redemption.
- **Comparison of Old and New Covenants:** The text draws parallels between the promises of the Old Covenant and the superior promises of the New Covenant, which offers not only physical protection but also spiritual salvation through Jesus Christ.

## Conclusion

"Healing Under the Old Covenant" illuminates the deep connections between obedience to divine laws and the health of the Israelites, serving as a precursor to the ultimate healing and salvation offered through Christ. The chapter emphasizes that while the Old Covenant was based on strict adherence to the law, the coming of Christ transforms this dynamic, offering grace and a more profound healing that encompasses both spiritual and physical realms.

## CHAPTER 4

# A BETTER COVENANT

### **Bible Verse**

Hebrews 8:6 NKJV "But now He has obtained a more excellent ministry, inasmuch as He is also Mediator of a better covenant, which was established on better promises."

### **Introduction**

"A Better Covenant" explores the superior nature of the New Covenant established through Jesus Christ compared to the Old Covenant. It discusses how the promises of healing and well-being are not only continued but enhanced in the New Covenant.

### **Word of Wisdom**

*"It only takes a little bit of leaven to spoil the entire lump, and that is what we have today." Chad Gonzales*

· · ·

## Main Theme

This chapter asserts that the New Covenant, through Christ's sacrifice, provides believers with unprecedented benefits, including a definitive promise of healing, which surpasses the conditional promises of the Old Covenant.

## Key Points

- The New Covenant offers promises that exceed those of the Old Covenant, including guaranteed health and longevity.
- Many Christians today struggle to experience the full benefits of the New Covenant due to misconceptions and altered teachings.
- Misinterpretations of Scripture over generations have muddied the original messages of Christ.
- Returning to the biblical text is essential to understand and reclaim the promises of the New Covenant.
- The integrity of the message from Jesus must be preserved to ensure its power and purity are not diluted.

## Key Themes

- **Superiority of the New Covenant:** The New Covenant is not only a continuation but an enhancement of the Old Covenant's promises, providing a fuller, more secure promise of health and prosperity based on

Christ's mediation and not on human obedience.
- **Challenges in Experiencing the Fullness of the New Covenant:** Despite the superior promises of the New Covenant, many believers do not experience its full benefits due to accumulated doctrinal errors, cultural shifts, and varied interpretations that have distorted the original message of Christ.
- **Impact of Miscommunication:** Like the telephone game, the message of healing and other promises of the New Covenant have been altered unintentionally over centuries, leading to a diluted and often ineffective understanding of what Jesus intended.
- **Necessity of Adherence to Biblical Text:** For believers to fully grasp and live out the benefits of the New Covenant, it is imperative to discard personal biases and previous misconceptions, focusing solely on the Scriptures as the ultimate authority.
- **Call to Return to the Source:** The chapter advocates for a return to the direct teachings of Jesus as recorded in the Scriptures, suggesting that a pure understanding of His words is crucial for living out the promises of the New Covenant effectively.

## Conclusion

"A Better Covenant" underscores the magnificence and breadth of what Jesus accomplished through His death and resurrection, offering believers not just a continuation of God's promises but an expansion with guaranteed healing and prosperity. The chapter calls for a reevaluation of personal and communal interpretations of Scripture to align closely with the truths Jesus imparted, ensuring that His followers can fully experience and manifest the benefits of the New Covenant.

# CHAPTER 5

# THE COVENANT OF GRACE

## Bible Verse

Psalm 105:37-43 NKJV "He also brought them out with silver and gold, and there was none feeble among His tribes. Egypt was glad when they departed, for the fear of them had fallen upon them. He spread a cloud for a covering, and fire to give light in the night."

## Introduction

"The Covenant of Grace" explores the transformative power of the New Covenant established through Jesus Christ, which is an improvement and fulfillment of the promises seen in the Old Covenant, particularly highlighted through the deliverance of the Israelites from Egypt.

## Word of Wisdom

*"What God did for them was not*

*based on their works, but based on God's grace." Chad Gonzales*

### Main Theme

This chapter delves into how the deliverance of the Israelites as described in the Old Testament prefigures the comprehensive salvation available through Christ under the New Covenant, which is not contingent on human works but on divine grace.

### Key Points

- The deliverance of the Israelites is a type and shadow of the salvation offered through Jesus Christ.
- The healing and prosperity of the Israelites were based on God's promise to Abraham, highlighting early examples of God's grace.
- The New Covenant offers better promises, emphasizing healing and a relationship not based on human effort but on Christ's mediation.
- Misinterpretations and cultural shifts have obscured the full understanding and experience of this covenant.
- The New Covenant promises not just to keep sickness at bay but to disconnect believers from sickness altogether.

### Key Themes

- **Historical Context and Typology:** The Old Testament events, particularly the deliverance from Egypt, serve as types and shadows of the greater salvation and healing that come through Christ. These events are not just historical but are spiritually instructive for understanding the breadth of God's redemptive plan.

- **Basis of the Covenant:** Unlike the Old Covenant, which was contingent on adherence to laws, the New Covenant is based on grace through faith in Christ, highlighting a shift from works to grace. This shift ensures that all who believe are recipients of God's promises irrespective of their actions.
- **Implications of Misunderstanding:** Modern Christians often do not experience the fullness of the New Covenant's promises due to historical misunderstandings and the dilution of the original messages of the gospel, much like errors introduced in the 'telephone game.'
- **Accessibility of the Promises:** Under the New Covenant, the promises of God, including healing and protection from sickness, are accessible to all believers through faith in Jesus Christ, rather than through ritual observance or moral perfection.
- **Role of Faith in Experience:** The chapter emphasizes that experiencing the benefits of the New Covenant requires a return to the foundational truths presented in Scripture, suggesting that a pure, faith-based approach to the gospel is essential for living out its promises.

## Conclusion

"The Covenant of Grace" reaffirms that the superior promises of the New Covenant, secured through the life, death, and resurrection of Jesus Christ, are accessible to all believers. It calls for a reexamination of personal and collective faith practices to align more closely with the biblical record, ensuring that believers fully embrace and live out the grace that is freely given, not earned.

## CHAPTER 6

## THE TRUE GOSPEL OF HEALING

### Bible Verse

Romans 5:17 NKJV "For if by the one man's offense death reigned through the one, much more those who receive abundance of grace and of the gift of righteousness will reign in life through the One, Jesus Christ."

### Introduction

"The True Gospel of Healing" challenges conventional teachings on healing within the church by revisiting the fundamental promises of the New Covenant in Christ, emphasizing that true healing is not merely physical but a complete disconnection from the curse of sin.

### Word of Wisdom

*"You don't have to believe to receive what you already have!" Chad Gonzales*

## Main Theme

This chapter redefines the concept of healing in the Christian faith, asserting that under the New Covenant, believers are not just prevented from illness but are completely severed from its root—sin, which is the true source of death and sickness.

## Key Points

- Under the Old Covenant, obedience was required to prevent sickness, whereas the New Covenant offers a permanent solution based on Christ's righteousness.
- Death reigned from Adam until Moses, but Christ's righteousness brings life.
- Jesus fundamentally changed our connection from sin (and thus death) to grace (and thus life).
- The traditional church often teaches about healing as something to be attained rather than a state of being.
- Believers are not just healed; they are transformed into new creations who live above the curse of sickness.

## Key Themes

- **Connection and Flow of Life vs. Death:** The concept of electrical flow is used metaphorically to describe how believers were previously connected to a flow of death through Adam's sin but are now connected to life through Christ. Just as a breaker can stop the flow of electricity, Christ's sacrifice permanently disconnects believers from sin and its consequences.

- **Healing as a Birthright Under the New Covenant:** Healing should be understood not as a conditional promise contingent upon behavior or faith but as an intrinsic aspect of the believer's new identity in Christ. It is not about 'getting' healed; it is about living out the health and wholeness that has already been granted through Jesus.
- **Misunderstandings in Modern Christian Teachings:** The modern interpretation of healing within many Christian circles is critiqued for being incomplete and misleading, focusing too much on healing from sickness rather than living in the health provided by Christ's atonement.
- **Biblical Foundation for Healing:** Key scriptures from Romans and Isaiah underscore that Jesus' atonement dealt with the root cause—sin, thereby nullifying its byproducts, including sickness. This theological foundation insists that where sin has been vanquished, sickness cannot legally persist.
- **Practical Application of Theological Truths:** The chapter encourages believers to embrace their new reality under the New Covenant. It argues that understanding one's identity in Christ as a new creation fundamentally changes the believer's experience and expectation of health.

## Conclusion

"The True Gospel of Healing" urges believers to shift their paradigm from seeking healing to living out the fullness of health and life promised in the New Covenant. It calls for a return to biblical truths about sin, righteousness, and healing, suggesting that a deeper understanding of these themes will lead to a more victorious and healthy life for all believers.

## CHAPTER 7

# THE REAL MEANING OF 1 PETER 2:24

### Bible Verse

1 Peter 2:24 NKJV "Who Himself bore our sins in His own body on the tree, that we, having died to sins, might live for righteousness—by whose stripes you were healed."

### Introduction

This chapter addresses the common misunderstandings surrounding 1 Peter 2:24, emphasizing that God's declaration of healing extends beyond physical ailments to include a complete liberation from the spiritual root of sickness—sin.

### Word of Wisdom

*"Sickness is a spiritual thing that manifests physically."* Chad Gonzales

## Main Theme

The chapter explores the deeper, often overlooked spiritual implications of healing in scripture, arguing that true healing as promised in the Bible involves a total severance from the source of all corruption—sin.

## Key Points

- God's declaration "You were healed" encompasses a complete severance from the root cause of sickness, which is sin.
- Our union with Christ means we share in His death to sin and, consequently, to the infirmities it brings.
- Righteousness, which we inherit through Christ, inherently includes healing.
- Misinterpretations of biblical texts have led to a reduced understanding of God's comprehensive plan for our well-being.
- True healing as described in the Bible means not just recovery from illness but an inherent immunity to it, established through our spiritual rebirth.

## Key Themes

- **Comprehensive Healing Beyond Physical Ailments:** Healing in the biblical context is not limited to physical recovery but is a complete and preemptive liberation from the possibility of disease.

This stems from our spiritual renewal and disconnection from sin through Christ's sacrifice.
- **Spiritual Nature of Sickness:** Sickness is portrayed not merely as a physical condition but as a manifestation of spiritual maladies. Just as sin has spiritual origins, so too does sickness, and healing must address this root to be effective.
- **Misinterpretation of Scripture:** Many Christians have misinterpreted scriptures like 1 Peter 2:24 to mean that God provides healing after sickness occurs. However, the true biblical promise is of a state where sickness cannot take hold due to the removal of sin.
- **Righteousness as a Shield Against Disease:** Righteousness, bestowed upon us through Jesus Christ, acts not just as a moral guide but as a protective barrier against sickness. This divine protection is inherent and continuous, not contingent on repeated acts of faith.
- **Implications for Christian Living:** Understanding the full scope of healing promised in the Bible should transform Christian living, encouraging believers to live in the confidence of their divine health and focusing on maintaining their spiritual connection to Christ rather than fearing illness.

## Conclusion

"The Real Meaning of 1 Peter 2:24" urges believers to embrace a more profound understanding of healing, which is not about battling sickness but about living in the freedom from sin and its consequences, including disease. This chapter calls for a shift in perspective from seeking healing to acknowledging and living out the wholeness that is already granted through our covenant with Christ.

## CHAPTER 8

## THE DAY YOU BECAME ALIVE

**Bible Verse**

2 Corinthians 5:17 NKJV "Therefore, if anyone is in Christ, he is a new creation; old things have passed away; behold, all things have become new."

**Introduction**

This chapter explores the transformation that occurs when one becomes a new creation in Christ, emphasizing the profound spiritual renewal that transcends mere physical existence.

**Word of Wisdom**

*"You must view sickness as no longer a possibility for you. Why? You are disconnected, and it can't flow anymore."*
*Chad Gonzales*

## Main Theme

The chapter underscores the real implications of being "born again," highlighting that this new life in Christ is not only about going to heaven but experiencing a quality of life on earth that reflects our spiritual rebirth and disconnection from the realm of sin and its consequences, including sickness.

## Key Points

- Being born again means we become a completely new, superior creation, not just reformed versions of our old selves.
- Our new identity in Christ disconnects us from our old life dominated by sin and its effects, including disease.
- Through Christ's resurrection, we also walk in a newness of life, mirroring His sinless and sickness-free existence.
- The spiritual reality of our new life in Christ means that the physical symptoms of the old sinful nature, like sickness, should no longer dominate.
- Understanding and embracing our new identity in Christ is essential for living out the fullness of this new life.
- Paul's teachings in Romans stress the importance of considering ourselves truly dead to sin and alive to God.

SUMMARY OF NEVER BE SICK AGAIN

## Key Themes

- **Transformation Beyond the Physical:** When we are born again, our transformation is profound and comprehensive, impacting our spiritual, emotional, and physical realities. This change is rooted in our new identity that aligns us with Christ's life and disassociates us from the life of sin.
- **New Creation as Superior Existence:** As new creations, we are not just refurbished old selves but entirely new beings who share in the divine nature of Christ. This newness is superior not only in moral quality but in life quality, embodying freedom from sin's dominion and its byproducts.
- **The Practical Outworking of New Life:** Living as a new creation involves daily acknowledging and operating in our new reality, which includes freedom from sickness. This requires a mindset shift from seeing ourselves as vulnerable to disease to recognizing our divine health in Christ.
- **Sin's Consequences Severed:** Just as sin introduced sickness and death into the world, our new life in Christ completely severs us from these consequences. This severance is not partial but total, ensuring that we live in the fullness of health and life as intended by God.
- **Living Out Our Heavenly Citizenship:** Our existence now mirrors Christ's heavenly life, not bound by earthly

limitations or ailments. As believers, we are called to manifest this heavenly reality here on earth, demonstrating what it means to be fully alive in Christ.

## Conclusion

"The Day You Became Alive" invites believers to radically redefine their understanding of salvation and healing, urging them to embrace their new identity in Christ, which guarantees a life free from sin and its consequences, including sickness. This chapter challenges believers to not only anticipate eternal life in heaven but to experience a vibrant, healthy, and supernatural life here and now, fully aligned with our status as new creations in Christ.

## CHAPTER 9

## MADE PERFECT

### Bible Verse

Hebrews 10:14 NKJV "For by one offering He has perfected forever those who are being sanctified."

### Introduction

This chapter delves into the transformative power of Christ's sacrifice, which not only redeems but also perfects us, establishing a new covenant where our innate flaws and sins are permanently addressed.

### Word of Wisdom

*"Even in the midst of your mess, you are still like the Messiah!" Chad Gonzales*

### Main Theme

"Made Perfect" explores how the sacrifice of Jesus Christ transcended the temporary measures of the old covenant, achieving a permanent state of perfection for believers that influences every aspect of their lives, including their health.

## Key Points

• Jesus's sacrifice was a permanent solution to the temporary fixes of the old covenant.

• Through Christ, believers are made perfect and complete, lacking nothing.

• Our perfection in Christ is not contingent upon our actions but is an inherent aspect of our new identity.

• Believers are forever righteous and perfect in God's eyes, regardless of ongoing sanctification.

• This divine perfection extends beyond spiritual aspects to influence physical health and wholeness.

## Key Themes

- **The Nature of Our Perfection:** In Christ, we are not just improved versions of ourselves; we are entirely new creations, made perfect through His sacrifice. This perfection is comprehensive, addressing our spiritual, physical, and moral imperfections.
- **The Finality of Christ's Sacrifice:** Unlike the repeated sacrifices of the old covenant, Christ's one-time sacrifice permanently establishes our righteousness and perfection. This act forever disconnects us from the sinful lineage of Adam, aligning us instead with the sinless nature of Christ.

- **Living in Recognized Perfection:** Although we continue to grow in spiritual maturity, our fundamental nature as believers is permanently perfected. This means that our mistakes and growth processes do not diminish our perfect standing before God.
- **Implications for Healing and Health:** Our state of being perfected in Christ directly impacts our physical health. Since we are disconnected from sin—the spiritual root of sickness—our bodies too should reflect this sanctified, healthful state.
- **Eternal Perspective on Righteousness:** Our perfection is eternal and unchanging because it is grounded not in our fluctuating faithfulness but in Christ's steadfast sacrifice. This eternal perspective should reshape how we view our identity, health, and daily living.

## Conclusion

The ninth chapter, "Made Perfect," reaffirms that believers are not striving for perfection but are living from a place of divine perfection, accomplished by Christ and imputed to us through faith. This understanding shifts the paradigm from battling for victory over sin and sickness to walking in the victory already won, where sickness no longer has a place, and perfect health is a manifestation of our perfected spirit.

## CHAPTER 10

## FILLED WITH LIFE

**Bible Verse**
John 1:4 NKJV "In Him was life, and the life was the light of men."

**Introduction**

"Filled with Life" examines the transition from spiritual death to life through Christ's redemption, highlighting the profound shift from Adam's disconnection to our reconnection with God's eternal life.

**Word of Wisdom**

*"Because Jesus was a possessor of life, then He could also give it away whenever He wanted to!" Chad Gonzales*

**Main Theme**

The chapter delves into the concept that through Christ, believers are not just restored but are imbued with the life-giving spirit of God, transforming them into new beings with divine life.

## Key Points

• Adam's sin resulted in spiritual death and a disconnection from God's life.

• Jesus, referred to as the last Adam, came to restore what the first Adam lost.

• Believers are now unified with God through Christ, filled with divine life.

• This divine life is not just for spiritual wellness but extends to physical health.

• The life of God within us is meant to overflow, impacting others around us.

## Key Themes

- **Transformation through Christ:** The life of God, which Adam lost through sin, has been restored in believers through Christ. This life is not merely an abstract spiritual concept but a tangible presence that influences physical and spiritual wellness.
- **Eternal Life as Present Reality:** The divine life within us is not waiting to be activated in the afterlife but is a current reality that believers can experience and manifest in their daily lives. This life provides not only salvation but also healing and restoration.
- **Jesus as the Life-Giver:** Just as physical traits are passed down genetically, spiritual

life, or the lack thereof, was passed down from Adam. Jesus, however, came to instill a new genetic lineage, spiritually speaking, where life, not death, is inherited.
- **Impact of Divine Life on Health:** The indwelling life of God acts as a divine immune system. This spiritual vitality is designed to repel sickness, demonstrating that healing is not a sporadic miracle but a constant state of being for the believer.
- **Living Out the Fullness of Life:** Believers are called to not only experience this life but to actively demonstrate it. The life of God within us should manifest as health, vitality, and an overflow that impacts the environment and people around us.

## Conclusion

Chapter 10 of "Filled with Life" redefines the believer's experience as one of dynamic and continuous interaction with the divine. It challenges Christians to recognize and operate in the reality of the eternal life they possess now, which actively transforms both their spiritual and physical existence.

## CHAPTER 11

## THE FLOW IN YOU

**Bible Verse**

John 7:38 NKJV "He who believes in Me, as the Scripture has said, out of his heart will flow rivers of living water."

**Introduction**

"The Flow in You" explores the concept of the divine life of God flowing within believers, empowering their spirits to dominate both soul and body, resulting in divine health and vitality.

**Word of Wisdom**

*"The water I give will become in him a fountain springing up into everlasting life."*
*— Jesus*

## Main Theme

This chapter underscores the transformative power of the life of God within believers, explaining how this divine essence not only revives but continually sustains and flows through them to bring about healing and wholeness.

## Key Points

- The life of God was breathed into man at creation, making him a living being.

- Our bodies are designed to respond to the spirit, which is supposed to be filled with the life of God.

- Jesus taught that the life He gives becomes a perpetual source of vitality within us.

- This divine life is meant to flow from believers affecting not only themselves but also those around them.

- Understanding and acknowledging the indwelling life of God is crucial for manifesting divine health.

## Key Themes

- **Divine Design and Original Intent:**
  God's original design was for humans to live with His life flowing within them, which was disrupted by sin but restored through Christ. This life of God within us is meant to be a constant source of health and vitality, transforming our physical reality.

- **Spiritual Authority Over Physical Reality:** As believers filled with the life of God, our spirits are intended to exert influence over our bodies. This divine life is not passive but actively works to bring our bodies into alignment with God's design for health and wholeness.
- **Perpetual Source of Divine Life:** Jesus' discussions with the Samaritan woman and other teachings highlight that the life He imparts to believers is not a temporary fix but a perpetual source of rejuvenation that springs up into everlasting life.
- **Healing as an Outflow of Divine Life:** The life within us is not only for our spiritual edification but also manifests physically as healing. This internal divine flow is so potent that it not only maintains personal health but also has the power to affect healing in others.
- **Revelation and Recognition of Divine Indwelling:** The key to unlocking the flow of this divine life is the revelation and acknowledgment of its presence within us. Believers must understand that they carry within them not just the potential for but the certainty of divine health and life.

## Conclusion

"The Flow in You" emphasizes the believer's role as a carrier of God's life, destined to manifest divine attributes physically and spiritually. It invites readers to shift their perception from seeking external divine interventions to recognizing and activating the powerful flow of life already present within them due to their union with Christ.

## CHAPTER 12

# WHO DO YOU THINK YOU ARE?

### Bible Verse

2 Corinthians 5:17 AMPC "Therefore if any person is [ingrafted] in Christ (the Messiah) he is a new creation (a new creature altogether); the old [previous moral and spiritual condition] has passed away. Behold, the fresh and new has come!"

### Introduction

This chapter delves into the critical importance of understanding our identity in Christ, emphasizing that many believers struggle because they do not fully grasp who they are as new creations, free from sin and alive in God's righteousness.

### Word of Wisdom

*"If you don't know who you are, you will not know what you have; your position*

*determines your possession." Chad Gonzales*

## Main Theme

The text explores how the misunderstanding of our identity in Christ is a primary obstacle to living a fulfilled Christian life, drawing a parallel with the first temptations in Eden, which centered on identity.

## Key Points

• Understanding our identity in Christ is fundamental to Christian living.

• Satan's primary tactic is to challenge and distort our understanding of our identity.

• Our new identity in Christ is as a new creation, entirely transformed and renewed.

• Recognizing ourselves in Christ changes how we view challenges and access God's power.

• True Christian identity is not about behavior modification but embracing a new existence in Christ.

• As new creations, we should identify with Christ's righteousness and authority, not our past sinful selves.

## Key Themes

- **Historical Context of Identity Challenges:** The narrative starts with Eve's temptation, highlighting that the confusion about our godly identity isn't a new issue but a fundamental challenge dating back to Eden. This theme is mirrored in the temptations faced by Jesus, demonstrating the continuity of this challenge across biblical history.
- **Christ's Temptation and Our Victory:** In Christ's response to Satan's temptations, we see a model for asserting our identity in God. Christ's firm knowledge of His identity as the Son of God provided the foundation for His victory, a blueprint for believers to emulate in overcoming their spiritual battles.
- **The Role of Scripture in Identity Confirmation:** The chapter emphasizes the transformative power of recognizing oneself in the scriptural promises and truths, particularly focusing on 2 Corinthians 5:17 as a pivotal verse that encapsulates the Christian's rebirth into a new identity.
- **Practical Implications of a Renewed Identity:** Understanding one's identity in Christ directly impacts one's ability to live out the fullness of life intended by God. It affects everyday interactions, decisions, and the ability to manifest the kingdom of God on Earth.
- **The Power of Righteousness:** The theme of righteousness is central to

understanding identity; it's not just a label but a real and operational aspect of our spiritual life, enabling us to manifest healing and divine power similarly to how Jesus did during His ministry.

## Conclusion

"Who Do You Think You Are?" calls for a profound shift in how believers view themselves in relation to Christ. By embracing our new identities as righteous and empowered by God, we can live out our divine heritage and walk in the authority and victory that has been granted to us through Jesus Christ. This shift is not just theological but requires a practical outworking that changes how we live daily.

## CHAPTER 13

# RECEIVING YOUR HEALING IS FOR THE SINNER

### Bible Verse

1 Peter 2:24 NKJV "Who Himself bore our sins in His own body on the tree, that we, having died to sins, might live for righteousness—by whose stripes you were healed."

### Introduction

This chapter challenges the traditional understanding of healing within the Christian community, emphasizing that healing is already granted through our identity in Christ rather than something we need to receive afresh.

### Word of Wisdom

*"In Christ, we are not receivers; we are releasers." Chad Gonzales*

## Main Theme

The chapter asserts that Christians already possess healing because of their new identity in Christ, contrasting this with the sinner who needs to receive healing as they do not have this inherent power.

## Key Points

• Healing is included in our salvation; it's not something we wait to receive but something we already possess.

• The traditional church often incorrectly teaches Christians to seek healing as if they don't already have it.

• Misunderstandings about healing often stem from a lack of identity awareness in Christ.

• Paul's letters focus on living out our new identity, not seeking to receive what we already have.

• True understanding of our identity simplifies our approach to divine health.

• Shifting perspective from needing to receive to realizing we already possess can lead to spontaneous manifestations of healing.

## Key Themes

- **Identity and Healing Misconceptions:** The chapter addresses the common misconceptions within the church regarding healing, stressing that many Christians struggle with sickness

because they view themselves as needing to receive healing, rather than understanding it as a part of their identity in Christ. This perspective shift is vital for realizing the fullness of health that belongs to believers.
- **Theological Foundation for Healing:** It argues that biblical passages like 1 Peter 2:24, often cited to encourage faith for healing, actually affirm that healing is already an accomplished fact for believers, not a conditional promise. This understanding should fundamentally change how healing ministry is approached and taught.
- **Practical Implications of Identity Recognition:** By recognizing their identity in Christ, believers can change how they interact with their own health challenges. Knowing that healing is already a granted state can lead to greater faith and less anxiety about health issues.
- **Contrasting Roles of Sinners and Saints in Healing:** The chapter contrasts the role of sinners, who need to receive healing, with saints, who only need to manifest what is already theirs. This distinction is crucial for empowering believers to live out their divine health.
- **Instruction on Walking in Healing:** The absence of teachings on how to receive healing in Paul's epistles is highlighted to affirm that healing should be recognized as an inherent aspect of the believer's life, not as a separate blessing to be sought.

## Conclusion

"Receiving Your Healing is for the Sinner" emphasizes that understanding our identity as new creations in Christ is crucial for manifesting the healing that is already ours. The chapter encourages believers to shift their focus from seeking to receive healing to acknowledging and releasing the healing power that resides within them due to their righteous status in Christ. This shift in understanding can lead to a more effective and faith-filled approach to divine health and spiritual life.

## CHAPTER 14

# YOU ARE THE BODY OF CHRIST

### Bible Verse

1 Corinthians 12:27 NKJV "Now you are the body of Christ, and members individually."

### Introduction

This chapter explores the profound connection between Christ as the head and believers as the body, emphasizing the continuous flow of life and power from Christ to His followers.

### Word of Wisdom

*"I am not praying or singing like others, 'Jesus, don't pass me by.' I'm not praying for God to show up or the Holy Spirit to fill me up or pour out His power. I am a branch divinely connected to the*

*Vine and receiving the fullness of His life every second of my life." Chad Gonzales*

## Main Theme

The unity between Christ and believers is likened to the anatomical relationship between a head and its body, illustrating that everything flowing in Christ also flows through His followers.

## Key Points

• Christ is the head of the Church; believers collectively and individually are His body.

• Each member of the body of Christ plays a unique and vital role, yet all share the same life that flows from Christ.

• Spiritual gifts and callings are distributed among the members to fulfill God's mission on Earth.

• Believers should see themselves as carriers and conduits of Christ's fullness and divine power.

• The health of the spiritual body should mirror the physical—free from sin and sickness.

## Key Themes

- **Connection and Flow from Christ:**
  Every believer, regardless of their role, is connected to Christ and receives His life.

This spiritual truth should govern how individuals view their capabilities and spiritual health, reinforcing that they possess everything necessary for life and godliness through their connection to Christ.

- **Role of Individual Believers Within the Body:** While the body of Christ is vast, each member has a crucial function. Understanding this helps believers recognize their worth and the importance of their contributions to the Kingdom of God, regardless of how visible or significant those contributions might seem.
- **Power and Authority of Believers:** As extensions of Christ on earth, believers are endowed with the authority to perform not only humanitarian deeds but also supernatural acts. This includes healing, a testament to the life of Christ flowing through them, challenging believers to step into their calling with boldness.
- **Identity and Self-Perception:** The chapter challenges believers to rethink how they see themselves in relation to Christ. It encourages viewing themselves not just as servants doing good but as powerful agents of Christ's life and healing, capable of affecting supernatural change in the world.
- **Theological Implications for Divine Health:** By emphasizing that sickness and sin are both alien to the body of Christ, the text calls for a radical reassessment of how believers handle sickness within the

church. It promotes a shift in mindset from accepting sickness as inevitable to confronting and overcoming it through the divine life provided by Christ.

## Conclusion

"You Are the Body of Christ" calls believers to a higher understanding of their identity and union with Christ. It urges them to embrace their role as His physical representation on earth, fully equipped with His power and authority to bring about change and manifest His kingdom. The chapter encourages a bold reevaluation of traditional teachings on healing and divine health, advocating for a robust, faith-filled practice that aligns with the believers' true nature as the embodiment of Christ Himself.

## CHAPTER 15

## DON'T GET CHEATED

### Bible Verse

Colossians 2:6-10 NKJV "As you therefore have received Christ Jesus the Lord, so walk in Him, rooted and built up in Him and established in the faith, as you have been taught, abounding in it with thanksgiving."

### Introduction

This chapter delves into the spiritual realm where Christians, unlike sinners, often find themselves cheated out of the blessings that rightfully belong to them through Christ. It explores the subtle yet pervasive ways believers can be misled away from the fullness of their inheritance in Christ.

### Word of Wisdom

*"Whatever your opinions and beliefs may be about the Christian life, they have to be filtered through Christ. Look at Him*

*for who He is at the right hand of God right now; if those opinions and beliefs aren't true for Him, they aren't true for you either!" Chad Gonzales*

## Main Theme

Christians often miss out on the full blessings of their spiritual inheritance not because these blessings are unavailable but because they are deceived into settling for less through worldly principles, human traditions, and flawed philosophies.

## Key Points

• Christians are entitled to all spiritual blessings in Heaven through Christ.

• Misguidance through human philosophy and traditions can lead believers astray.

• The standards set by Jesus Christ are often compromised by worldly logic.

• Believers should constantly affirm and walk in their identity in Christ to avoid being cheated.

• Traditional practices can become idols that detract from the purity and power of the gospel.

## Key Themes

- **The Reality of Spiritual Cheating:** Believers are frequently cheated out of their spiritual inheritance because they adopt worldly standards and values that conflict with the truths of the gospel. This cheating happens subtly through the acceptance of secular norms and the dilution of divine standards.
- **Dangers of Philosophical and Traditional Deceptions:** The chapter warns against the influence of human philosophy and empty deceit, which are often disguised as wisdom but actually lead believers away from the completeness found in Christ. These deceptions are contrasted with the truth and simplicity of the gospel, which offers a fuller, more powerful way of life.
- **Christ as the Standard:** The chapter emphasizes that Jesus Christ, glorified and seated at the right hand of God, is the benchmark for believers' lives. Anything that does not align with His life and power is considered a deviation from the truth and a form of cheating oneself out of what Christ has secured.
- **Importance of Right Beliefs and Practices:** It is crucial for believers to examine and align their beliefs and practices strictly with what is reflected in the life and teachings of Jesus. Practices rooted in tradition rather than truth can lead to spiritual stagnation and loss.

- **Call to Recognize and Reject Worldly Norms:** The text challenges Christians to reject worldly norms regarding health, aging, and spiritual power, advocating for a perspective that mirrors the victorious and supernatural life Christ led and promised to His followers.

## Conclusion

"Don't Get Cheated" calls for a radical return to gospel purity, urging believers to claim their full inheritance through a deep, unwavering connection to Christ. It encourages a vigilant rejection of any teaching or practice that diminishes the power and presence of Christ in the believer's life, fostering a community that truly lives out its divine nature and calling.

## CHAPTER 16

## OUR BELIEF IN SICKNESS

### Bible Verse

Romans 12:2 NKJV "And do not be conformed to this world, but be transformed by the renewing of your mind, that you may prove what is that good and acceptable and perfect will of God."

### Introduction

This chapter challenges the Christian community's acceptance of sickness as a normal part of life, arguing that such beliefs are contrary to the divine health promised in the gospel. It emphasizes the power of belief in shaping our experiences, especially concerning health.

### Word of Wisdom

*"Satan knows that as a believer, you are already healed because you are righteous. He also knows that if he can get you*

*working to get what you already have, you'll let go of what you have because you don't think you have it." Chad Gonzales*

## Main Theme

The central theme of this chapter is the call for Christians to reject the world's normative beliefs about sickness and to embrace the biblical promise of divine health, fundamentally altering their perceptions and expectations regarding illness.

## Key Points

• Belief in sickness opens the door to illness in the Christian life.

• The biblical call is for transformation through mind renewal, focusing on divine health.

• Christians often prepare for sickness due to worldly conditioning.

• The teachings on healing in many churches often assume sickness as inevitable.

• There is a disconnect between the biblical promises of health and the Church's expectations.

• Christians should challenge and change their beliefs about health based on Christ's life.

## Key Themes

- **The Power of Renewed Beliefs:** The chapter underscores the necessity of renewing the mind with the realities of Christ's life in Heaven, not earthly limitations. This renewal is essential for Christians to manifest the fullness of divine health as intended by God.
- **Rejecting Worldly Norms:** It criticizes the church's acceptance of the world's views on health and aging, which often leads to a resigned acceptance of sickness. Instead, it calls for a radical alignment with the health and vitality that is evident in Jesus Christ.
- **The Role of Righteous Identity in Health:** The text connects the believer's righteousness with their right to divine health, arguing that being right with God includes being free from sickness, a stark contrast to the world's acceptance of disease as inevitable.
- **Practical Faith versus Theoretical Acceptance:** There is a critique of how the church often teaches about healing—focusing on managing sickness rather than living in the full health promised by God. This practical application of faith is missing in many Christian teachings.
- **Cultural and Traditional Influences on Belief Systems:** The influence of cultural and traditional misconceptions within the church is explored, showing how these can detract from the powerful

truths of Scripture regarding healing and health.

## Conclusion

"Our Belief in Sickness" calls Christians to a higher standard of living that aligns with the heavenly realities of Christ's life, urging them to reject passive acceptance of illness. By shifting focus from earthly norms to divine promises, believers can fully manifest the health and vitality that their faith in Christ entitles them to.

## CHAPTER 17

# A NEW KINGDOM

### Bible Verse

Colossians 1:13-14 TPT "He has rescued us completely from the tyrannical rule of darkness and has translated us into the kingdom realm of his beloved Son. For in the Son all our sins are canceled and we have the release of redemption through his very blood."

### Introduction

This chapter emphasizes the radical transformation Christians undergo through salvation, shifting from the kingdom of darkness to the Kingdom of God, where sickness and disease are non-existent.

### Word of Wisdom

*"Jesus completely delivered us and then brought us over into His Kingdom."*
*Chad Gonzales*

## Main Theme

The main theme explores the reality of living under the new covenant of God's Kingdom on earth, emphasizing that the norms of heaven—where no sickness or pain exist—should be the believer's norms on earth.

## Key Points

- Believers are already citizens of God's Kingdom, where divine health is normal.

- Redemption through Christ translates us into a life free from sin's byproducts like sickness.

- Earthly challenges shouldn't change our heavenly reality.

- The life expectancy and quality seen in biblical figures like Moses challenge modern expectations of aging and health.

- True belief in God's promises leads to a life markedly different from worldly experiences.

## Key Themes

- **Heavenly Standards on Earth:** The chapter stresses that what is normal in heaven should be normal for believers on earth. Since there is no sickness in heaven, believers should not accept it as part of their earthly life.
- **Transformative Power of Salvation:** Salvation is portrayed not just as a rescue

from sin, but a complete transformation that relocates believers into a new realm of existence—God's Kingdom—with all its benefits, including health and wholeness.
- **Disconnect from Worldly Norms:** The text urges believers to disconnect their expectations from worldly norms, especially regarding health and aging, advocating for a mindset that expects divine health as a standard.
- **Biblical Examples as Models:** The longevity and vitality of biblical figures like Moses are presented as models for what believers should expect in their own lives, challenging the acceptance of deterioration with age.
- **Renewing the Mind:** There is a strong emphasis on the necessity of renewing the mind to align with Kingdom realities, which dictates that believers live free from the diseases recognized in the world.

## Conclusion

"A New Kingdom" encourages believers to live out the full implications of their citizenship in God's Kingdom here and now, by embracing a life free from the ailments considered normal in the world. It calls for a radical shift in mindset from earthly to heavenly norms, especially in the area of health.

# CHAPTER 18

# SUBSTITUTING BRASS FOR GOLD

## Bible Verse

Mark 16:15-18 NKJV "And He said to them, 'Go into all the world and preach the gospel to every creature. He who believes and is baptized will be saved; but he who does not believe will be condemned. And these signs will follow those who believe: In My name they will cast out demons; they will speak with new tongues; they will take up serpents; and if they drink anything deadly, it will by no means hurt them; they will lay hands on the sick, and they will recover.'"

## Introduction

This chapter challenges the common practice of Christians seeking healing primarily from other believers rather than extending healing to non-believers, as originally intended in the Great Commission.

## Word of Wisdom

*"We have substituted brass for gold by changing the focus of healing from its divine intent." Chad Gonzales*

## Main Theme

The main theme discusses the misplaced focus in contemporary Christian practice where believers often seek healing from one another rather than empowering each believer to heal others, especially non-believers, as a testament to God's power.

## Key Points

- Jesus commissioned believers to heal as a sign to non-believers.

- Historically, most healings in the Bible were directed at non-believers.

- James 5 references a rare instance where elders heal a gravely sick believer.

- Believers often substitute lesser experiences (brass) for the fullness of God's promise (gold).

- The early Church likely saw fewer sick among them due to their understanding of and living in divine health.

## Key Themes

- **Misdirected Healing Practices:** The chapter critiques the modern church's focus on healing within the congregation rather than as an evangelical tool aimed at non-believers, suggesting this shift has weakened the church's outreach and testimony.

- **Biblical Precedence for Healing:** It points out that the New Testament primarily records instances of healing as a sign for non-believers, with very few instances involving believers, suggesting that divine health was more common among early Christians than it is today.
- **The Role of Faith and Authority:** Discusses how the church has moved away from the authority given by Christ to every believer, encouraging a dependency on "special" individuals rather than recognizing the inherent power given to all believers.
- **Cultural Misalignment with Scriptural Intentions:** The chapter suggests that cultural shifts within the church have led to practices not fully aligned with Scripture, particularly in how healing and miracles are perceived and practiced.
- **Empowering Believers to Manifest Divine Health:** Encourages a return to teaching believers about their identity in Christ, which includes the authority to heal and be in health, reducing the church's dependency on healing ministries.

## Conclusion

"Substituting Brass for Gold" calls for a

reformation in the church's approach to divine healing, urging believers to embrace and exercise their God-given authority to heal as a testament to the gospel, particularly to non-believers, thereby restoring the church's foundational mission as outlined by Christ.

## CHAPTER 19

# GENERATIONAL CURSES AND YOUR BLOODLINE

### Bible Verse

Galatians 3:13 NKJV "Christ has redeemed us from the curse of the law, having become a curse for us (for it is written, 'Cursed is everyone who hangs on a tree'),"

### Introduction

This chapter addresses the misconception among Christians regarding generational curses, emphasizing the complete redemption provided through Christ that negates any ancestral curses once one accepts Jesus.

### Word of Wisdom

*"Friend, Jesus redeemed your bloodline when He redeemed you. Jesus' past is now your past, and God the Father is the beginning of your bloodline."*

## Main Theme

The chapter refutes the belief in generational curses among Christians by underscoring the transformative power of redemption through Christ, which severs ties with any past curses and establishes a new lineage rooted in divine blessing.

## Key Points

• The concept of generational curses is not applicable to Christians who are new creations in Christ.

• Believers are fully redeemed from the curse of the law through Christ's sacrifice.

• Teachings on generational curses misunderstand and misapply scriptural truths.

• Union with Christ fundamentally changes one's spiritual lineage and heritage.

• Redemption in Christ means complete freedom from all curses, including generational ones.

## Key Themes

- **Misapplication of Old Testament Laws:** The belief in generational curses among Christians often stems from a misinterpretation of Old Testament scriptures, particularly Exodus 20:5, which does not apply under the new covenant established through Jesus Christ.
- **Redemption and New Creation Reality:** By becoming believers, individuals are reborn

into a new spiritual lineage with God as their Father, making the concept of needing to 'redeem one's bloodline' irrelevant and contrary to the truths of the New Testament.
- **Theological Implications of Generational Curses:** Teaching that believers must break generational curses undermines the completeness of Christ's redemptive work, suggesting that His sacrifice was insufficient.
- **Practical Effects of Erroneous Beliefs:** Belief in generational curses can lead Christians to live in unnecessary fear and bondage, diverting focus from the freedom and authority granted through faith in Christ.
- **Corrective Teaching on Spiritual Heritage:** The chapter encourages a shift in teaching towards understanding our identity and heritage in Christ, promoting a life free from the fears of inherited curses and focused on inherited blessings.

## Conclusion

"Generational Curses and Your Bloodline" challenges and aims to correct the erroneous teachings about generational curses in the Christian community by emphasizing the all-encompassing redemption through Christ. It encourages believers to embrace their new identity in Christ, which is free from any curses and rich in generational blessings.

## CHAPTER 20

# SATAN ISN'T TRESPASSING ON YOUR BODY

### Bible Verse
1 Peter 5:8 NKJV "Be sober, be vigilant; because your adversary the devil walks about like a roaring lion, seeking whom he may devour."

### Introduction

This chapter challenges the common Christian belief that Satan can involuntarily affect believers' bodies with sickness, emphasizing the doctrinal truth that Satan cannot trespass where he has not been given permission.

### Word of Wisdom

*"Satan cannot trespass against a righteous person. Righteous people are masters over Satan; he can't do whatever*

*he wants because he must have our permission." Chad Gonzales*

## Main Theme

The central theme explores the concept that Satan has no authority to invade or afflict a believer's body without their consent, debunking the myth of involuntary demonic influence on believers' physical well-being.

## Key Points

- Satan's interaction with humanity involves temptation, not coercion.

- Righteous individuals, like Jesus and Eve before the fall, cannot be involuntarily controlled by Satan.

- Believers have full authority over their own bodies and spiritual state.

- The concept of Satan trespassing is a misunderstanding of biblical teachings on authority and dominion.

- Understanding and exercising one's authority in Christ is crucial to maintaining spiritual and physical health.

## Key Themes

- **Misconceptions of Satan's Power:** The belief that Satan can directly inflict

sickness upon individuals without their spiritual consent is a significant error, contradicting the scriptural depiction of Satan as a tempter who must rely on deception rather than force.
- **Biblical Examples of Temptation:** Both historical (Eve in Genesis) and allegorical (Jesus in the wilderness) examples in scripture demonstrate that Satan's power is limited to what is permitted by the individuals he tempts, emphasizing the need for vigilance and spiritual maturity in resisting his ploys.
- **Authority of the Believer:** Christians possess comprehensive authority over their lives, including health and spiritual state, through their union with Christ. This authority renders the concept of involuntary demonic influence null.
- **Role of Consent in Spiritual Warfare:** Understanding that spiritual warfare involves consent clarifies the believer's role in maintaining their health and spiritual purity by actively choosing to align with God's word and resist demonic influences.
- **Practical Application of Authority:** Teaching believers to recognize and exercise their God-given authority can prevent many of the spiritual and physical ailments mistakenly attributed to demonic attacks, changing the focus from fear to empowerment.

## Conclusion

"Satan Isn't Trespassing on Your Body" corrects a

common doctrinal error by affirming that Satan has no power to affect believers without their permission. It calls for a reevaluation of teachings on spiritual warfare, emphasizing the empowerment of believers through their inherent authority in Christ. This shift from fear to authoritative living in Christ aims to equip believers with the knowledge and tools to effectively stand against any form of demonic deception or attack.

CHAPTER 21

# WHATEVER HAS YOUR IMAGINATION HAS YOUR FAITH

### Bible Verse
3 John 2 NKJV "Beloved, I pray that you may prosper in all things and be in health, just as your soul prospers."

### Introduction

This chapter delves into the significant impact of imagination on faith, illustrating how our mental and emotional engagement can directly influence our physical and spiritual well-being.

### Word of Wisdom

*"Whatever has your imagination has your faith." Chad Gonzales*

## Main Theme

The primary focus is on the powerful role of imagination in shaping our beliefs and outcomes, particularly in terms of health and spiritual life, emphasizing that what we mentally entertain can manifest in our lives.

## Key Points

- Imagination directly influences physical and spiritual realities.

- Thoughts introduced by Satan are merely suggestions, not compulsions.

- Eve's deception by Satan highlights the power of manipulated imagination.

- Righteous individuals have control over their spiritual and physical state.

- Renewing the mind is essential for maintaining spiritual and physical health.

## Key Themes

- **Link Between Imagination and Physical Health:** There is a profound connection between our mental state and our physical health, as our body often follows the lead of our mind and emotions, making the renewal of our mind through spiritual truths essential for overall well-being.
- **Satan's Limited Influence:** Satan's influence over individuals is restricted to

planting thoughts, which requires personal acceptance to take effect. Understanding this limitation empowers believers to reject these mental intrusions effectively.
- **Importance of Guarding the Mind:** Just as our physical body needs protection from harm, our imagination needs to be guarded against negative influences that can lead to spiritual and physical ailments.
- **Role of Imagination in Spiritual Warfare:** Imagination is not just a passive faculty but an active battlefield where spiritual victories and defeats can occur, highlighting the importance of aligning our imaginations with God's truth.
- **Practical Steps to Leverage Imagination Positively:** By intentionally focusing our imagination on divine truths and promises, we can fortify our faith and manifest the reality of these truths in our lives, leading to improved spiritual and physical health.

## Conclusion

"Whatever Has Your Imagination Has Your Faith" underscores the necessity of managing our imagination to align with biblical truths, stressing that our spiritual and physical health is significantly influenced by what we choose to mentally entertain. By nurturing a godly imagination, believers can safeguard their health and enhance their spiritual life, living out the fullness of their divine inheritance in Christ.

# CHAPTER 22

# STAY CONNECTED TO THE SOURCE

## Bible Verse

John 15:5 TPT "I am the sprouting vine and you're my branches. As you live in union with me as your source, fruitfulness will stream from within you—but when you live separated from me you are powerless."

## Introduction

This chapter emphasizes the importance of maintaining a continuous and conscious connection to Christ, the source of all spiritual power and health, underscoring that true healing and spiritual effectiveness flow from this vital relationship rather than from individual efforts.

## Word of Wisdom

*"Without Me, you can do nothing and you are powerless." - Jesus*

SUMMARY OF NEVER BE SICK AGAIN

## Main Theme

The central theme discusses the futility of trying to achieve spiritual outcomes, including healing, through human efforts alone and highlights the critical need for believers to rely wholly on their union with Christ.

## Key Points

- Faith and authority in Christ are foundational but not sufficient alone.

- Actions like confession and scriptural engagement are meant to enhance fellowship with God, not replace reliance on His grace.

- True spiritual effectiveness stems from a continuous and deep relationship with Christ.

- Maintaining a conscious awareness of Christ is crucial for spiritual health.

- Spiritual decline begins when our awareness of God's presence diminishes.

## Key Themes

- **The Role of Grace in Spiritual Practices:** Grace is not just the initiator but also the sustainer of our spiritual life; it provides everything needed for life and godliness through our union with Christ. Efforts to work for what grace has provided are contrary to the principle of resting in Christ's finished work.

- **Constant Awareness of Christ's Presence:** The quality of our spiritual life is directly proportional to our awareness of Christ's presence. As believers, we must cultivate a continuous consciousness of being in Christ to access the spiritual resources available to us.
- **Abiding in Christ as a Continuous Act:** Jesus' command to abide in Him involves a deliberate choice to remain connected to Him at all times. This connection is not automatic and requires intentional focus and commitment to maintain.
- **Fellowship with God Through the Word and Prayer:** Engaging with the Scriptures and praying in the Spirit are not mere religious activities but avenues to deepen our communion with God. This fellowship is crucial for nurturing our faith and enabling it to grow.
- **Encounters with God as Transformative Experiences:** Regular, profound encounters with God are necessary for maintaining and boosting our spiritual vitality. These encounters help reinforce our identity in Christ and empower us to live out our faith effectively.

## Conclusion

"Stay Connected to the Source" serves as a vital reminder that the essence of Christian living is not found in religious activities or self-driven efforts but in a dynamic and living relationship with Christ. By focusing on deepening our relationship with Him, we enable His life to flow through us, resulting in spiritual fruitfulness and divine health.

# CHAPTER 23

# WHEN CHRISTIANS ARE SICK

### Bible Verse

Romans 6:10-11 NKJV "For the death that He died, He died to sin [sickness] once for all; but the life that He lives, He lives to God. Likewise you also, reckon yourselves to be dead indeed to sin [sickness], but alive to God in Christ Jesus our Lord."

### Introduction

This chapter addresses why many Christians still suffer from illnesses despite the biblical promise of divine health, suggesting that the disconnect lies in our perceptions and actions regarding sickness.

### Word of Wisdom

*"We must properly discern the Lord's body and see ourselves for who He is."*
*Chad Gonzales*

## Main Theme

The key theme is the power of belief and the importance of aligning our imaginations with the reality of Christ's victory over sin and sickness.

## Key Points

- Believing in the possibility of sickness can make us susceptible to it.

- Failure to control our imaginations can lead to negative health outcomes.

- Physical neglect of our bodies can contribute to illness.

- Condemnation and a disconnect from our identity in Christ can lead to sickness.

- Maintaining a constant awareness of God's presence is crucial for health.

## Key Themes

- **Belief Systems and Health:** Our health is often a reflection of our beliefs. If we consider sickness as a possibility, we align ourselves with that reality, thereby opening the door to illness despite Christ's provision for health.
- **Imagination and Physical Health:** An uncontrolled imagination can be detrimental. Focusing our thoughts on divine health rather than disease is essential, as what occupies our mind tends to manifest in our life.

- **Physical Stewardship and Divine Health:** Taking care of the physical body is not just about avoiding sickness; it's a spiritual duty. Neglecting this temple can hinder the flow of divine life within us.
- **Identity in Christ and Health Outcomes:** Recognizing and maintaining our identity in Christ is vital. When we forget our union with Christ, we become vulnerable to condemnation, which can manifest as physical illness.
- **Practical Steps to Maintaining Health:** Engaging in practices that strengthen our awareness of God—such as communion, meditation on scriptural truths, and spiritual fellowship—helps keep us aligned with the truth of our divine health.

## Conclusion

"When Christians Are Sick" underscores the necessity of a renewed mind and a spirit-led life to walk in the fullness of health that Christ has provided. It calls believers to actively reject the lies of the enemy regarding sickness, maintain their spiritual health through consistent communion with God, and live out their faith boldly, embodying the victory over sickness that is already theirs in Christ.

## CHAPTER 24

## ACCIDENTS AND INJURIES

### Bible Verse
Psalm 91:9-12 NLT
"If you make the Lord your refuge, if you make the Most High your shelter, no evil will conquer you; no plague will come near your home. For He will order His angels to protect you wherever you go. They will hold you up with their hands so you won't even hurt your foot on a stone."

### Introduction

This chapter delves into the often-overlooked topic of accidents and injuries in the life of a believer. It challenges the assumption that accidents are random, emphasizing the protective guidance of the Holy Spirit and the role of divine healing, even when injuries occur due to human error or disobedience.

## Word of Wisdom

*"The Holy Spirit knows the end from the beginning, and He wants to protect you." Chad Gonzales*

## Main Theme

Accidents and injuries can often be avoided by listening to the Holy Spirit's guidance, but even in moments of disobedience, God's mercy and healing are always available.

## Key Points

• Accidents happen when believers fail to follow the Holy Spirit's guidance.

• Psalm 91 promises divine protection for those who trust and abide in God.

• The Holy Spirit acts as a tour guide in life, leading believers to avoid harm.

• Even when injuries occur due to human error, God's healing power is always accessible.

• Learning to hear and obey the Holy Spirit can help believers live accident-free lives.

• God's goodness ensures restoration even when mistakes lead to injury.

## Key Themes

- Psalm 91 guarantees that those who trust in the Lord and abide in His presence will experience protection from harm. This includes freedom from sickness, accidents, and injuries, provided believers remain sensitive to the Holy Spirit's leading.
- The Holy Spirit acts as a personal guide, providing warnings and directions to avoid dangerous situations. Whether it's a delayed departure or a specific decision, obedience to these promptings ensures safety and divine alignment.
- Personal stories illustrate how disobedience to the Spirit's promptings can lead to avoidable accidents and injuries. These anecdotes highlight the importance of spiritual sensitivity and the consequences of neglecting divine warnings.
- Even when believers disobey and suffer injuries, God's grace provides healing. His life-giving power is always present within, ready to restore health and wholeness, even when the injury results from human stubbornness.
- Developing a habit of listening to the Holy Spirit requires daily intentionality. As believers grow in their relationship with God, they can navigate life's challenges without fear of accidents or harm, relying on divine guidance and protection.

## Conclusion

This chapter reinforces the truth that God's plan for believers includes divine protection from accidents and injuries. By listening to the Holy Spirit and staying connected to His guidance, believers can live untouchable lives. Even in moments of failure, God's healing power is available to restore what has been lost, proving His faithfulness and mercy time and again.

## CHAPTER 25

## FOOD AND DRUGS

### Bible Verse
1 Corinthians 6:19 NKJV
"Or do you not know that your body is the temple of the Holy Spirit who is in you, whom you have from God, and you are not your own?"

### Introduction

This chapter focuses on the responsibility believers have to care for their bodies, the temple of God, by making informed choices about food and health. It addresses the role of nutrition, exercise, and self-control, highlighting how modern diets and reliance on medications often compromise divine health. The discussion emphasizes returning to God's design for sustenance and stewardship over our physical well-being.

### Word of Wisdom

*"Christians are doing this to themselves, and then, after contracting dis-*

*eases, we want to start using our authority against the devil. What we need to do is use our authority over our desires and exercise self-control." Chad Gonzales*

## Main Theme

Believers are called to honor God by caring for their bodies through proper nutrition, exercise, and self-discipline, aligning their physical health with spiritual stewardship.

## Key Points

• Your body is the temple of the Holy Spirit, and you are responsible for its care.

• Many diseases today are self-inflicted due to poor dietary and lifestyle choices.

• God created natural, whole foods to sustain our health, not laboratory-modified alternatives.

• Ultra-processed foods and excessive sugar intake contribute to chronic illnesses.

• Exercise, proper nutrition, and sleep are essential for maintaining health and preventing disease.

• Relying solely on medications without lifestyle changes often leads to managing symptoms rather than true healing.

## Key Themes

- **Responsibility for the Temple of God:** As believers, our bodies are not our own but are the temple of the Holy Spirit. Caring for them is a spiritual act of worship and a demonstration of stewardship, reflecting God's design for health and wholeness.
- **The Impact of Food on Health:** The increase in diseases such as diabetes, heart disease, and cancer correlates directly with processed and nutrient-deficient foods. God's design for food, as outlined in Genesis, provides all the nutrients our bodies need for optimal function.
- **The Role of Self-Control in Health:** Overcoming unhealthy habits requires the fruit of self-control. Believers are called to exercise authority over their cravings, making conscious choices to align their lifestyles with God's will for their health.
- **The Misuse of Medications:** While modern medicine has its place, reliance on prescription drugs often treats symptoms rather than addressing root causes. True healing involves aligning physical care with God's principles for health, which includes nutrition and lifestyle changes.
- **The Need for a Lifestyle Change in the Church:** Many health issues plaguing Christians are preventable through better choices. A commitment to proper nutrition, regular exercise, and honoring God with our bodies can lead to improved

quality of life and fewer unnecessary prayers for healing.

## Conclusion

Believers must take a proactive approach to health by recognizing their bodies as temples of the Holy Spirit and making choices that honor God. By returning to God's design for food and embracing self-discipline in lifestyle habits, Christians can experience divine health. As the author emphasizes, "It costs way less to be healthy than it does to be sick." Let us commit to aligning our physical care with our spiritual values, ensuring that our lives reflect the glory of God in every aspect.

Harrison House is a Spirit-filled, Word of Faith Christian publisher dedicated to spreading the message of faith, hope, and love through our wide range of inspiring publications. Committed to the messages that highlight the power of the Word and Spirit, we provide books, devotionals, and study guides that empower believers to live victorious, faith-filled lives.

Our resources are designed to help readers grow spiritually, strengthen their faith, and experience the transformative power of God's Word. Harrison House is passionate about equipping Christians with the tools they need to fulfill their divine purpose and impact the world for Christ.